WOULD YOU RATHER

BOOK FOR KIDS

By SUNNY BOOKS
Publishing

WOULD YOU RATHER...

eat a turkey sandwich

~ or ~

a chicken sandwich?

ride a skateboard

~ or ~

a bike?

WOULD YOU RATHER...

visit every country
in the World

~ or ~

be able to play any
musical instrument?

control the outcome
of any coin flip

~ or ~

be unbeatable at
rock, paper, scissors?

WOULD YOU RATHER...

be able to
type faster than anyone

~ **or** ~

speak faster than anyone?

have a private movie theater

~ **or** ~

your own private arcade?

WOULD YOU RATHER...

be a cyborg

~ **or** ~

a robot?

ride in a hang glider

~ **or** ~

skydive?

WOULD YOU RATHER...

every vegetable you eat taste
like candy but still be healthy

~ or ~

all water you drink taste like a
different delicious beverage
every time you drink it?

be really good at skateboarding

~ or ~

really good at any
video game you tried?

WOULD YOU RATHER...

lay in a bathtub
filled with worms

~ or ~

lay in a bathtub
filled with beetles

live next to a theme park

~ or ~

next to a zoo?

WOULD YOU RATHER...

have a room with whiteboard
walls that you can draw on

~ or ~

a room where the whole
ceiling is one big skylight?

have a house with
trampoline floors

~ or ~

a house with
aquarium floors?

WOULD YOU RATHER...

learn to surf

~ **or** ~

learn to ride a skateboard?

eat your favorite food every day

~ **or** ~

find 5 dollars under
your pillow every morning?

WOULD YOU RATHER...

have a pet penguin

~ or ~

have a pet Komodo dragon?

be able to talk to animals

~ or ~

be able to fly?

WOULD YOU RATHER...

own a restaurant

~ **or** ~

be a chef?

have a pet dinosaur
of your choosing

~ **or** ~

a dragon the size of a dog?

WOULD YOU RATHER...

have an amazing tree house

~ or ~

your whole yard be a trampoline?

have a slide that goes from your
home's roof to the ground

~ or ~

be able to change and control
what color the lights
are in your home?

WOULD YOU RATHER...

be a famous musician

~ **or** ~

a famous business owner?

play in a giant mud puddle

~ **or** ~

a pool?

WOULD YOU RATHER...

have your favorite artist perform
a private show just for you

~ or ~

perform on stage next
to your favorite artist
for thousands of people?

be too hot

~ or ~

too cold?

WOULD YOU RATHER...

have 100$ now

~ **or** ~

1000$ in a year?

have a real triceratops

~ **or** ~

a robot triceratops?

WOULD YOU RATHER...

have everything
you draw become real

~ **or** ~

become a superhero
of your choice?

be given every Lego set
that was ever made

~ **or** ~

get every new Lego set
that comes out for free?

WOULD YOU RATHER...

go to the beach

~ **or** ~

go to the zoo?

get a new pair of shoes

~ **or** ~

a jacket?

WOULD YOU RATHER...

read a book

~ **or** ~

read a magazine?

be the fastest swimmer on earth

~ **or** ~

the third fastest
runner on earth?

WOULD YOU RATHER...

drink orange juice

~ **or** ~

milk?

go camping

~ **or** ~

stay in a hotel room?

WOULD YOU RATHER...

have one eye in the
middle of your head

~ **or** ~

two noses?

have a mermaid as a friend

~ **or** ~

a god fairy as a friend?

WOULD YOU RATHER...

live in a castle

~ **or** ~

a spaceship
traveling far from earth?

go to the Moon

~ **or** ~

stay on Earth forever?

WOULD YOU RATHER...

play soccer

~ **or** ~

baseball?

ride a camel

~ **or** ~

ride a horse?

WOULD YOU RATHER...

be amazing at
drawing and painting

~ or ~

amazing at photography?

ride a skateboard?

~ or ~

rollerblade?

WOULD YOU RATHER...

get up early

~ **or** ~

stay up late?

be able to eat any
spicy food without a problem

~ **or** ~

never be bitten by
another mosquito?

WOULD YOU RATHER...

have to take a bath/shower
but still always smell nice
~ or ~
never have to get another
shot but still be healthy?

be able to learn everything
in a book by putting it under
your pillow while you slept

~ or ~

be able to control
your dreams every night?

WOULD YOU RATHER...

be able to see new colors
that no other people could see

~ or ~

be able to hear things
that no other humans can hear?

move to a country and city of
your choice

~ or ~

stay in your own country but
not be able to decide
where you moved?

WOULD YOU RATHER...

have pancakes every day
~ or ~
pizza every day

drive a race car
~ or ~
fly a helicopter?

WOULD YOU RATHER...

be unable to control
how fast you talk

~ or ~

unable to control
how loud you talk?

be rich and unknown

~ or ~

be famous and have enough money,
but not be rich?

WOULD YOU RATHER...

live in a house in the forest
where there aren't many people around
~ or ~
live in a city with
lots of people around?

dance
~ or ~
draw?

WOULD YOU RATHER...

be a detective

~ or ~

a pilot ?

go skiing

~ or ~

go to a water park?

WOULD YOU RATHER...

fly a kite

~ or ~

swing on a swing?

play hide and seek

~ or ~

dodgeball?

WOULD YOU RATHER...

have a full suit of armor

~ **or** ~

a horse?

be a wizard

~ **or** ~

a superhero?

WOULD YOU RATHER...

sail a boat

~ **or** ~

ride in a hang glider?

brush your teeth with soap

~ **or** ~

drink sour milk?

WOULD YOU RATHER...

be a famous inventor

~ **or** ~

a famous writer?

do school work as a group

~ **or** ~

by yourself?

WOULD YOU RATHER...

fly an airplane

~ **or** ~

drive a fire truck?

be a talented engineer

~ **or** ~

a talented scientist?

WOULD YOU RATHER...

spend the whole day
in a huge garden

~ or ~

spend the
whole day in a large museum?

be able to find anything]
that was lost

~ or ~

every time you touched
someone they would be unable to lie?

WOULD YOU RATHER...

be a babysitter

~ **or** ~

a dog sitter?

ride a bike

~ **or** ~

ride a kick scooter?

WOULD YOU RATHER...

work alone on a school project

~ **or** ~

work with others on a school project?

open one 5$ present every day

~ **or** ~

one big present that costs
between 100$ to 300$ once a month?

WOULD YOU RATHER...

have an unlimited supply of ice cream

~ or ~

a popular ice cream flavor
named after you?

live in a place that is always dust

~ or ~

always humid?

WOULD YOU RATHER...

be able to do flips
    and backflips
    ~ **or** ~
        break dance?

see a firework display

    ~ **or** ~

a circus performance?

WOULD YOU RATHER...

it be warm and raining

~ **or** ~

cold and snowing today?

be able to create
a new holiday

~ **or** ~

create a new sport?

WOULD YOU RATHER...

only be able to
walk on all fours

~ or ~

only be able to
walk sideways like a crab?

start a colony on
another planet

~ or ~

be the leader of
a small country on Earth?

WOULD YOU RATHER...

be able to see things that are
very far away, like binoculars

~ or ~

be able to see things
very close up, like a microscope?

be an incredibly fast swimmer

~ or ~

an incredibly fast runner?

WOULD YOU RATHER...

own an old-timey
pirate ship and crew

~ or ~

a private jet with
a pilot and infinite fuel?

be able to jump
as far as a kangaroo

~ or ~

hold your breath
as long as a whale?

WOULD YOU RATHER...

be able to
type/text very fast

~ **or** ~

be able to read really quickly?

randomly turn into a frog
for a day once a month

~ **or** ~

randomly turn into a bird
for a day once every week?

WOULD YOU RATHER...

be really good at math

~ **or** ~

eally good at sports?

be the author of a popular book

~ **or** ~

a musician in a band
who released a popular album?

WOULD YOU RATHER...

live in a house
shaped like a circle

~ **or** ~

a house shaped like a triangle?

live in a place with
a lot of trees

~ **or** ~

live in a place near the ocean?

WOULD YOU RATHER...

have your room redecorated
however you want

~ **or** ~

ten toys of your
choice (can be any price)?

have a magic carpet that flies

~ **or** ~

a see-through submarine?

WOULD YOU RATHER...

everything in your
house be one color

~ **or** ~

every single wall and
door be a different color?

visit the international
space station for a week

~ **or** ~

stay in an underwater
hotel for a week?

WOULD YOU RATHER...

have ninja-like skills

~ **or** ~

have a spy agent skills?

be able to control fire

~ **or** ~

water?

WOULD YOU RATHER...

have a new silly hat appear
in your closet every morning

~ **or** ~

a new pair of shoes appear
in your closet once a week?

be able to remember everything
you've ever seen and heard

~ **or** ~

be able to perfectly
imitate any voice you heard?

WOULD YOU RATHER...

drink every meal as a smoothie
~ or ~
never be able to eat
food that has been cooked?

meet your favorite celebrity
~ or ~
be on a TV show?

WOULD YOU RATHER...

be a master at origami
~ **or** ~
a master of
sleight of hand magic?

have a tail that
can't grab things

~ **or** ~

wings that can't fly?

WOULD YOU RATHER...

have a special room you
could fill with as many bubbles
as you want, anytime you want

~ or ~

have a slide that goes from
your roof to the ground?

dance in front of 1000 people

~ or ~

sing in front of 1000 people?

WOULD YOU RATHER...

ride a very big horse

~ **or** ~

a very small pony?

be able to shrink down to the size
of an ant any time you wanted to

~ **or** ~

be able to grow to the size of
a two-story building anytime
you wanted to?

WOULD YOU RATHER...

be able to move silently

~ or ~

have an incredibly
loud and scary voice?

be bulletproof

~ or ~

be able to survive
falls from any height?

WOULD YOU RATHER...

eat a whole raw onion

~ or ~

a whole lemon?

be incredibly luck
with average intelligence

~ or ~

incredibly smart
with average luck?

WOULD YOU RATHER...

be able to change color
to camouflage yourself

~ or ~

grow fifteen feet taller and shrink
back down whenever you wanted?

instantly become a grown up

~ or ~

stay the age you are now
for another two years?

WOULD YOU RATHER...

have a personal life-sized robot

~ or ~

a jetpack?

never have any homework

~ or ~

be paid 10$ per hour
for doing your homework?

WOULD YOU RATHER...

eat a bowl of spaghetti noodles
without sauce

~ or ~

a bowl of spaghetti sauce
without noodles?

have eyes that change color
depending on your mood

~ or ~

hair that changes color
depending on the temperature?

WOULD YOU RATHER...

eat an apple

~ **or** ~

an orange?

taste the best pizza that has
ever existed once but never again

~ **or** ~

have the 4th best pizza restaurant
in the world within delivery distance?

WOULD YOU RATHER...

go snorkeling on a reef

~ or ~

camping by a lake?

have an elephant-sized cat

~ or ~

a cat-sized elephant?

WOULD YOU RATHER...

take a math class

~ or ~

an art class?

play outdoors

~ or ~

indoors?

WOULD YOU RATHER...

eat broccoli flavored ice cream

~ **or** ~

meat flavored cookies?

eat one live nonpoisonous spider

~ **or** ~

have fifty nonpoisonous
spiders crawl on you all at once?

WOULD YOU RATHER...

live on a sailboat

~ or ~

in a cabin deep in the woods?

have an amazing tree house
with slides and three rooms

~ or ~

an amazing entertainment system
with a huge TV and every game console?

WOULD YOU RATHER...

eat a popsicle

~ **or** ~

a cupcake?

own a hot air balloon

~ **or** ~

an airboat?

WOULD YOU RATHER...

have a bubble gun that shoots
giant 5-foot bubbles
~ or ~
a bathtub-sized pile of Legos?

eat a worm
~ or ~
a grasshopper?

WOULD YOU RATHER...

have super strength
~ **or** ~
super speed?

never eat cheese again
~ **or** ~
never drink anything
sweet again?

WOULD YOU RATHER...

have your very own house
next to your parent's house

~ **or** ~

live with your parents in a
house that's twice the size
of the one you live in now?

have a cupcake

~ **or** ~

a piece of cake?

WOULD YOU RATHER...

be able to move wires
around with your mind
~ or ~
be able to turn any
carpeted floor into a
six-foot deep pool of water?

be able to speak any language but
not be able to read in any of them
~ or ~
read any language but not
be able to speak any of them?

WOULD YOU RATHER...

live in a house where all
the walls were made of glass

~ **or** ~

live in an underground house?

stay a kid until you turn 80

~ **or** ~

instantly turn 40?

WOULD YOU RATHER...

be able to watch any movies you
want a week before they are released

~ or ~

always know what will be
trendy before it becomes a trend?

be an athlete in the Summer Olympics

~ or ~

the Winter Olympics?

WOULD YOU RATHER...

be fluent in 10 languages

~ or ~

be able to code in 10 different
programming languages?

drive a police car

~ or ~

an ambulance?

WOULD YOU RATHER...

have a piggy bank that doubles
any money you put in it
~ or ~
find ten dollars under your
pillow every time you wake up?

own a mouse

~ or ~

a rat?

WOULD YOU RATHER...

rather live in a cave

~ or ~

a tree house?

do a book report

~ or ~

a science project
for a school assignment?

WOULD YOU RATHER...

have any book you wanted for free

~ **or** ~

be able to watch any
movie you wanted for free?

be able to play the piano

~ **or** ~

the guitar?

WOULD YOU RATHER...

be able to read lips

~ **or** ~

know sign language?

eat a hamburger

~ **or** ~

a hot dog?

WOULD YOU RATHER...

rather ride a roller coaster

~ or ~

see a movie?

be able to change the color of
anything with just a thought

~ or ~

know every language that
has ever been spoken on Earth?

WOULD YOU RATHER...

have super strong arms

~ or ~

super strong legs?

move to a different city

~ or ~

move to a different country?

WOULD YOU RATHER...

choose Instagram

~ or ~

Facebook?

be wildly popular on
the social media platform

~ or ~

your choice or have an
extremely popular podcast?

WOULD YOU RATHER...

be able to talk to animals

~ **or** ~

an Alien?

eat smores

~ **or** ~

cupcakes?

WOULD YOU RATHER...

ride in a hang glider

~ or ~

ride in a helicopter?

never have to sleep

~ or ~

never have to eat?

WOULD YOU RATHER...

be an amazing photographer

~ **or** ~

an amazing writer?

sneeze uncontrollably
for 15 minutes once every day

~ **or** ~

sneeze once every 3 minutes
of the day while you are awake?

WOULD YOU RATHER...

be able to remember everything
in every book you read

~ or ~

remember every
conversation you have?

have 10 mosquito bites

~ or ~

1 bee sting?

WOULD YOU RATHER...

be an actor/actress in a movie

~ or ~

a movie script writer?

be able to talk to dogs

~ or ~

cats?

WOULD YOU RATHER...

have a jetpack

~ **or** ~

a jet?

ride a roller coaster

~ **or** ~

go down a giant water slide?

WOULD YOU RATHER...

get every Lego set that
comes out for free

~ **or** ~

every new video game system
that comes out for free?

go on vacation to a new country
every summer vacation

~ **or** ~

get an extra three weeks
of summer break?

WOULD YOU RATHER...

go snow skiing

~ **or** ~

water skiing?

never be able to eat
any type meat again

~ **or** ~

never be able to eat things
with sugar in them?

WOULD YOU RATHER...

have no homework

~ **or** ~

no tests?

be able to control the length
of your hair with your mind

~ **or** ~

be able to control the length
of your fingernails with your mind?

WOULD YOU RATHER...

get to name a newly
discovered tree

~ or ~

a newly discovered spider?

swim in Jell-O

~ or ~

swim in Nutella?

WOULD YOU RATHER...

play on swings

~ **or** ~

play on a slide?

have the power to shrink things
to half their size

~ **or** ~

the power to enlarge
things to twice their size?

WOULD YOU RATHER...

live in a base under the ocean

~ or ~

a floating base in the sky?

not need to eat and
never be hungry

~ or ~

not need to drink and
never be thirsty?

WOULD YOU RATHER...

be the fastest kid
at your school

~ or ~

the smartest kid
at your school?

be a scientist

~ or ~

be the boss of a company?

WOULD YOU RATHER...

have a magic freezer
that always has all your
favorite ice cream flavors
~ or ~
one that has a different
ice cream flavor every time
you open the door?

have a very powerful telescope

~ or ~

a very powerful microscope?

WOULD YOU RATHER...

hang out for an hour
with 10 puppies

~ or ~

10 kittens?

be able to change colors
like a chameleon

~ or ~

hold your breath
underwater for an hour?

WOULD YOU RATHER...

go to the doctor for a shot

~ or ~

the dentist to get
a cavity filled?

be able to make plants
grow very quickly

~ or ~

be able to make it
rain whenever you wanted?

WOULD YOU RATHER...

be a falcon

~ **or** ~

a dolphin?

be able to read minds

~ **or** ~

see one day into the future?

WOULD YOU RATHER...

have fireworks go off
every evening for an hour

~ or ~

have Christmas
three times a year?

eat a bowl of spaghetti
that was just one long noodle

~ or ~

eat ice cream
launched from a catapult?

WOULD YOU RATHER...

watch a two-hour movie

~ **or** ~

watch two hours of shows?

go to the doctor

~ **or** ~

dentist?

WOULD YOU RATHER...

eat a dead bug

~ **or** ~

a live worm?

get good grades

~ **or** ~

be good at sports?

WOULD YOU RATHER...

sneeze cheese

~ **or** ~

have your tears be
chocolate flavored?

have 500 spiders in your bedroom

~ **or** ~

1000 grasshoppers in the
rest of the house?

Made in the USA
Columbia, SC
01 June 2022

61184153R10057